EXITS AND ENTRANCES

Poetry by Naomi Long Madgett

Songs to a Phantom Nightingale (1941)
One and the Many (1956)
Star by Star (1965, 1970)
Pink Ladies in the Afternoon (1972)
Exits and Entrances (1978)
Phantom Nightingale: Juvenilia (1981)

Exits and Entrances

new poems by

Naomi Long Madgett

Drawings by Beverley Rose Enright

LOTUS PRESS DETROIT

Copyright © 1978
by Naomi Long Madgett

First Edition
Second Printing, 1986

International Standard Book Number 0-916418-13-8
Library of Congress Catalog Number 77-91712

Manufactured in the United States of America

LOTUS PRESS, INC.
P. O. Box 21607
DETROIT, MICHIGAN 48221

For Leonard
lovingly

Some of these poems were first published in *The Black Star, A Change of Weather: Midwest Women Poets, Deep Rivers, Ebony, Echoes from the Moon, First World, Ocarina, South and West,* and *World Order.* Permission to reprint them is gratefully acknowledged.

Contents

FAMILY PORTRAIT

"Our birth is but a sleep and a forgetting:
The Soul that rises with us, our life's Star,
  Hath had elsewhere its setting,
    and cometh from afar...."
                              (*Wordsworth*)

Where was I, Mother, in the photograph?
    "Why, child, you were not even born."
Who is that sitting on my father's knee?
    "Your brother, child."
                              But Mother,
What baby's softness is that cuddled there
So tenderly against your breast?
    "Your other brother, child."
But Mother, where was I?
    "You were not born yet, silly goose."
But Mother, where *was* I?

ALBUM: PHOTO 2

(For Clarence and Wil)

Before the depression
My father bought a used green Chandler.
One day he drove it right across the yard
And parked it on the scant grass
Our baseball games had spared
Between the clothesline posts
(First and second base)
To take some photographs.

My mother, awkward camera boxed in dainty hands,
Captured my brothers in plaid lumberjackets
And stiff new knickerbockers,
Their soap-sheen faces beaming toward futurity.

My face is there too, frowning from the driver's window
Between my brothers' shoulders:
One eye, a forehead, and a wilted braid of hair.

I do not remember the car.
My jacket was too tight, and the buttons
Were on the wrong side.

SATURDAY NIGHT AT THE PARSONAGE

The rolls are on the radiator rising
and the kitchen warm with the aroma
of Mama's good chicken dressing. All the shoes
are polished and the verses memorized
for Sunday school. Daddy's robe is pressed
and his white collar starched and laid beside
the open Bible where he has marked his text.
We line up for the ritual of baths
no longer ordinary but baptism
as sure as any in Jordan's chilly waters.
Just before prayers and bed, I get to lick
the spoon and run my finger around the bowl
of batter from the gingerbread now browning
in the oven. *Oh, what a foretaste,*
what a foretaste of glory divine!

DEACON MORGAN

His artificial feet calumped in holy rhythm
down the center aisle of Calvary Baptist Church
to Deacons' Row in front.
He knelt to pray before he took his chair.

Little and popeyed in our pew,
we never ceased to marvel
that he could strut when he got happy,
walk the narrow straitly,
and even drive a car.
Surely an understanding Jesus
had laid His hands on him.

Oh, lowlier than angels,
more visible than Holy Ghost,
he was our credible atonement,
our certainty of Paradise
who, having sinned we thought
and had his limbs cut off for punishment,
was welcome still in the abundant household
of a loving Father.

MUFFLEJAW, I REMEMBER YOU

(For Lillian on North Clinton Street)

Small greenspring puffs of breath balloon into
absurd enormities of furred and furry days

although I have no whiskers to guide me
safely through amorphous dark
and my paws were never cushioned for
such silent and mysterious sojourn as you knew.

It was a long time ago
but I will be here when your Maltese spirit
searches me out again.

Superimposed upon my spindly ten-year legs
cotton-ribbed against New Jersey winters
is laid the strength my sturdy limbs have learned.
I know where I stash my armor and why
and I no longer flinch nor run.

Oh, I remember you, Mufflejaw, gray
against the blackwhite days,
your ancient feline face muted,
inscrutable in a wisdom of
more ages than my mind could span.

KIN

(For Jill)

Something has passed between us more than blood,
keener than bone that locks us into rhythms
of chin and cheek and brow. When diamond glints
of sun bounce from your mountains
my wings in shadow soar;
when rutted clay entraps your feet
my own steps slog in kindred snares.

Leaves of one vine entwine us utterly
nourished by juices of a common earth.
Your seasons shake me louder than the sounds of chance,
deeper than solitudes of birth.

FANTASIA

(For Jill)

1. Silver one year was a broomstick from the kitchen
   and you rode him like the ranger
   that you were. No stranger to the prairie,
   you pursued relentlessly bank robber, cattle-rustler,
   quick on the draw of your six-shooter. Till
   one day you questioned, "Kemo sabe,
   what makes Tonto talk that funny way?
   How come he don't speak regular?"

   Then you became an Indian princess,
   Beautiful Dark Feather, child
   of the reservation who had once been
   creature of the forest and the rain,
   now victim of the land that mothered you.
   Oh, praise the sun and moon, my little one,
   and wonder why you live in darkness!
   Oh, sing your lament of hunger amid
   the abundance of the earth!

2. Another year you fled the terrors of the Creature
   from the Black Lagoon, swam
   through thrilling murk of monster-fear
   to splash triumphant on sun-flooded shore.

   Sun dimmed and spotlight rose
   to flood another stage. Pony-tailed,
   properly obsequious, you bowed
   before your royal father, King of Siam.
   When the applause quieted and you returned
   to ordinary day,
   new grace and glory clung to one
   who for a little while had been
   child of a king.

3. Reading *Mein Kampf* behind your eighth grade history book,
   graduating to philosophies you knew
   would revolutionize the world,
   you came again as Rose of Spanish Harlem,
   street-corner girl bathed in radiant beauty
   of a distant island: dancing on sidewalks
   under streetlight's arc: searching for moonmagic lost
   or never known: needing,
   needing other people, needing love . . .

   Came crashing through a paper sky—
   hit ground and splattered in the wind
   like Humpty Dumpty—
   somehow gathered and rejoined the fragments
   into imperfect whole that would never, ever
   grow smooth again
   over its cataclysmic pain.

4. Fell in love with Black Orpheus . . .
   danced through carnival with rediscovered joy . . .
   gave away new clothes you'd saved so long to buy
       to Rio's hillside poor—
           wouldn't rob them of their dignity
           by snapping pictures . . .

   Then you were the Girl
   from Ipanema, frolicking
   in the Brazilian sunshine
   of your independence, tossing
   pebbles at old ghosts still lurking
   along the seashore, finding
   your self in the golden faces
   that taught you how to phrase
   old thoughts anew in foreign tongue.

5. You discovered Africa another year
   dancing to rhythms you remembered as your own,
   sculptured your features from Sahara sands
   and found them beautiful. Force
   of her rivers bore you home at last
   to who you are.
   Little brown mama with Afro'd hair
   and infant waking in your arms,
   the cycle of discovery is passing
   into a larger circle now. The harvest
   you have gleaned from childhood's fantasies
   provides the seed for an expanded planting.
   Farmer of many dreams, you till the earth
   that gives my springtime dreams their second birth.

THE SILVER CORD

The minute hand of a defective clock
circles in perennial embrace
a faded crystal innocence.

Pinched by the limitations of an outgrown infancy,
small shoes bronzed into permanence of pain
stand motionless upon a marble mantel.

Time and its ornaments cannot disguise
the limp, raw cord still pulsing
with fresh severing.

Someone please tell her now
before it is too late
to tie the knot and let it fall away.

FIFTH STREET EXIT, RICHMOND

1. Leave the freeway at this point.
   Drive off where a chainlink fence
   separates the road from a patch of weeds
   and forces you past a row of ancient houses dying
   from the fever of progress. Hurry past.
   Proceed with cautious speed down Fifth Street
   to Main, beyond the place where death lurks, where
   airy ghosts peer through the dust of floor-long
   windows and scream with hollow voiceless mouths.

2. The phantom children are calling,
   they are calling my name.
   They are playing hide-and-seek
   by yellow streetlight and
   they cannot find me. I am busy
   chasing fireflies.
   The phantom children are calling,
   calling my name.

3. I could go back if I wanted to.
   I could join the dance again
   bouncing my feet with theirs
   on the sidewalk of uneven brick
   as they jump   jump
   and jump Jim Crow.

   I could learn again to make
   the swooping gesture
      Cotton needs a-pickin' so-o-o bad
   in rhythm with their song
   (graceless newcomer from the North
   but eager to be one with them).
      Cotton needs a-pickin' so-o-o bad
      I'm gonna pick all over this land.
   I *could* do it again.
   If I wanted to.

4. The clop-clop-clop of horses' hooves,
   the clatter of wagon wheels on cobblestones
   bring the street vendor to the shade
   of our magnolias.

   Above the horses' whinnying
   his cindery voice, half-song, half-wail,
   bellows, blasts across
   the heavy air.

   > *Get your fresh watermelon,*
   > *Sweet melon, cold melon,*
   > *Black-seeded juicy melon,*
   > *Ripe melon sweet.*

   Oh, the spicy redolence of summer!
   Oh, the freshfruit glories of Southern
   summertime!

   > *Watermelon, sweet melon,*
   > *Black-seeded fresh melon,*
   > *Come buy your watermelon,*
   > *Ripe melon sweet.*

5. Wil and Clarence and Dadie and Lew
   played mumble-de-peg by the curb, and Suzie
   whimpered and put up her hair in balls
   while Bubber chased me around the yard, and

   Grampa died and Bubber cried
   and knocked me down and gashed my head
   and Dadie's father stitched my wound
   and Sadie cut my hair that summer

   and seasons came and long years went
   and Richmond just kept coming back
   and we were grown before we guessed
   the wonder that those summers meant.

6. I wish I *could* go back
   to the cool green shuttered dark
   that hid us from the boisterous sun

   from the explosion of color and fragrance outside
   back into the cocoon

   back to the Concord grapes ripening
   in the arbor where the swing hung still
   patient   waiting   for the evening cool—

   afternoon baths and starched white
   eyelet dresses with blue sashes
   and patent leather shoes:

        Richmond summers chocolate
        as childhood's toothsomest delights.

   I wish I could.

7. Azalea petals fell for the last time
   one spring and tried in vain
   to fertilize this asphalt garden.
   The bricks crumbled and were hauled away,
   the green shutters fell to dust
   and where Grandma's white-pillared porch
   once welcomed Sunday callers
   a chainlink fence went up to mark an exit
   from Wherever, U.S.A., to Main Street, Richmond.

   Leave the freeway at this point and don't,
   oh, don't go back. Don't listen
   to the children's hollow voices
   chanting elegies to the whir
   of wheels turning, turning.

WASHERWOMAN

Time is
an old washerwoman
who scrubs away
the grit of memory
rinsing   wringing
hanging in the sun
to dry   till the garment
of experience becomes
soft and wearable.

CATASTROPHE

A ghostly moon cast chill shadows
across our sultry street,
spidery silver in an unfamiliar twilight.
Indoors the oppressive heat hung soggy
as wet clothing on a line.
We clustered on our porches, dumb,
waiting for the streetlights to come on,
half afraid they never would,
half fearing what they might reveal.

Silhouettes of dead trees that had not fallen
but would never bear another leaf,
skeletal buildings of naked steel and gaping windows
leaned red against the impending darkness
as children's games hung strangely suspended.
The weak light of a distant madness
engulfed us, but no one dared
to light a lamp.

CITY NIGHTS

(For Gertrude and Eddie)

My windows and doors are barred
against the intrusion of thieves.
The neighbors' dogs howl in pain
at the screech of sirens.
There is nothing you can tell me
about the city
I do not know.

On the front porch it is cool and quiet
after the high-pitched panic passes.
The windows across the street gleam
in the dark.
There is a faint suggestion of moon-shadow
above the golden street light.
The grandchildren are asleep upstairs
and we are happy for their presence.

The conversation comes around to Grampa Henry
thrown into the Detroit River by an Indian woman
seeking to save him from the sinking ship.
(Or was he the one who was the African prince
employed to oversee the chained slave-cargo,
preventing their rebellion, and for reward
set free?)
The family will never settle it; somebody lost
the history they had so carefully preserved.

Insurance rates are soaring.
It is not safe to walk the streets at night.
The news reports keep telling us the things
they need to say: The case
is hopeless.

But the front porch is cool and quiet.
The neighbors are dark and warm.
The grandchildren are upstairs dreaming
and we are happy for their presence.

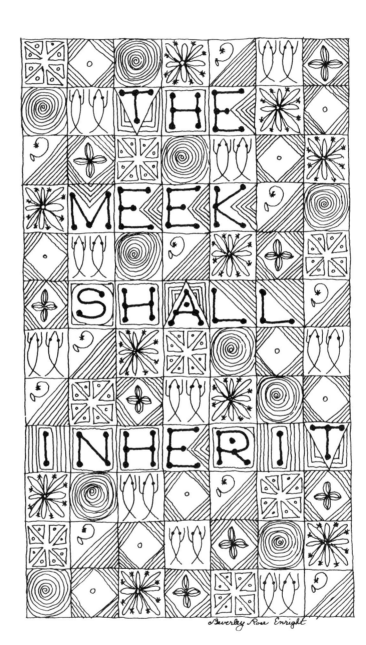

THE MEEK SHALL INHERIT

Beverley Rose Enright

THE SURVIVORS

(For Ishmael Reed)

Civilizations
die hard   like
old women
in the marketplace
grinding   their gums
mumbling their
years
     scarred beads
     of a tarnished
       rosary

If I should tell you who
the survivors will be
     you would not believe
       me
If I said, "The meek shall
     inherit,"
you would not understand
     who
       or
        how

It takes a burial more violent
than you are willing
to concede   to prove
     the point   but then
why try to prove the point
since anyhow
no one will ever claim
     the corpse
and no relations will be left
     to mourn

NOMEN

(To Femi Sodipo and my African-American ancestors)

"What's in a name?"
          (Shakespeare)

          My sunlight came pre-packaged
          from the corner store
          a few days old
          and always overpriced

          but somehow I brought it safely
          past thieves in dingy doorways
          beyond fly-spattered mailboxes
          with broken locks
                    to my father's many-mansioned home.

          Too many tombstones have been toppled,
          too many pigeons have already fouled
          the names and dates no longer legible.

          So I will keep the name my father gave me
          being neither anonymous nor poor
          and having no need to let myself be robbed
          a second time.

THE OLD WOMEN

They are young.
They do not understand
what the old women are saying.

They see the gnarled hands raised
and think they are praying.
They cannot see the weapons hung

between their fingers. When the mouths
gape and the rasping noises
crunch like dead leaves,

they laugh at the voices
they think are trying to sing.
They are young

and have not learned
the many faces of endurance, the furtive
triumphs earned through suffering.

IN SEARCH OF AUNT JEMIMA
(Alias Big Mama)

Everybody's looking for Big Mama,
spatula in hand and ample
table set for all of master's children,
serving generous portions
of forgiving love with open
gold-tooth smile.

Everybody needs to nestle in
her warm, full bosom, hear again
that throaty voice belt out
deep-valleyed lullabies of blackness
(shouting hosannas or moaning
blues for good man gone).

Where did Aunt Jemima go? And when
will she return to reassure us
that her delicious laughter
was innocent and wholesome to partake of
and no more subtle
and no more dangerous
than her pancakes?

MONDAY MORNING BLUES

All night my bed was rocky, all night nobody by my side;
My bed was cold and rocky, all night no good man by my side.
The radiator sputtered, the furnace gave a groan and died.

I woke up dreaming Friday, but Monday dragged me out of bed;
Yes, woke up dreaming Friday, Monday dragged me out of bed.
Was looking for a paycheck, mailman brought me bills instead.

Well, no one comes to see me, no one ever telephones;
Nobody but Misfortune visits me or telephones.
Wish I could find me something as lucky as a black cat's bones.

You may not see me smiling, still you'll never hear me cry;
Seldom see me smiling, never gonna hear me cry;
But I do a lot of laughing 'cause I'm too damn proud to die.

NEW DAY

"Keep a-inchin' along, keep-a inchin' along,
Jesus 'll come bye an' bye.
Keep a-inchin' along like a po' inchworm,
Jesus 'll come bye an' bye."
(Negro Spiritual)

She coaxes her fat in front of her
like a loaded market basket with defective wheels.
Then she pursues it, slowly catches up, and
the cycle begins again.
Every step is a hardship and a triumph.

As she inches her way along in my direction
I sense the stretchings and drawings of
her heavy years. I feel the thunderous
effort of her movement reverberating through
a wilderness of multiple betrayals.
As gently as I can, I say, "Good morning, Sister,"
as we come face to face, and wonder
if she can understand what I am saying.

Akua'ba fertility doll.
Ashanti, Ghana. Collection
of the poet, Detroit.

POINT OF VIEW

We took the trip together,
But all that she could see
Was elephants and leopards,
Uncaged and running free.

She hunted with a camera
Then followed with a gun,
Determined to enslave or kill
Whatever prize she won.

I saw a race of people
Whose bloodline flowed to me:
My heritage, their beauty,
Their cage, my history.

We winged our way together
Across the ocean's foam,
But she went on safari
While I went home.

A LITANY FOR AFRO-AMERICANS

Our ancestors called Thee by other names,
But Thou, O God, were with us
In the dawn of time.

    LORD, BE WITH US STILL.

From Ife and Timbuktu we came,
Crying to Thee in the agonies
Of the Middle Passage.

    WE CRY TO THEE TODAY.

In the confinement of our bodies' chains,
Our spirits nightly floated free.

    FREE OUR SPIRITS NOW, WE PRAY.

We watched the captors steal our names,
Our continuity, the richness of our heritage,
And we were naked and impotent
Against the evil of their power.
Other captors rob us still.

    TEACH US TO BE WATCHFUL, LORD,
    TEACH US TO BE STRONG.

Against false prophets,
Against destructive forces
That seek to divide us
And deny us the family of Thy spirit,
The family of *our* spirit,

    PROTECT US, O GOD,
    AND LEAD US IN THE WAY
    OF POWER THROUGH RIGHTEOUSNESS.
    AMEN.

PHILLIS

I hardly remember my mother's face now,
But I still feel
At my bosom a chill wind
Stirring strange longings for the sturdy back
I used to lean against for warmth and comfort
When I had grown too tall to ride.

And I am blinded by
The glint of sunlight
Striking golden fire from the flint
Of seafoamed rocks below me
On some island not too far from home.

After that, the only light I saw
Was a few wayward chinks of day
That somehow slanted into the airless tomb
Where chains confined me motionless to a dank wall.

Then the sun died and time went out completely.
In that new putrid helltrap of the dead
And dying, the stench
Of vomit, sweat, and feces
Mingled with the queasy motion
Of the ship until my senses failed me . . .

I do not know how many weeks or months
I neither thought nor felt, but I awoke
One night—or day, perhaps—
Revived by consciousness of sound.

Phillis Wheatley (1753-1784) was an American slave poet who came to this country
as a child from Senegal, West Africa.

                                                  I heard
The pounding of the waves against the shipside
And made believe its rhythm
Was the speech of tribal drums
Summoning in acute need the spirit
Of my ancestors. I dreamed I saw
Their carven images arrayed
In ceremonial austerity. I thought I heard
Their voices thundering an answer
To my supplication: "Hold fast.
Sur/vive   sur/vive   sur/*vive*!"
And then I slept again . . .

Once more the sunlight came, but not the same
As I remembered it. Now it sat silver-cold
Upon the indifferent New England coast. Still
It was good to see the sun at all.
And it was something
To find myself the bright dark mascot
Of a blind but well-intentioned host—
A toy, a curiosity, a child
Taking delight in anyone's attention
After so long a death.

As I grew older, it was not enough.
That native lifesong once again burst free,
Spilled over sands of my acquired rituals—
Urged me to match the tribal rhythms
That had so long sustained me, that must
Sustain me still. I learned to sing
A dual song:

> *My fathers will forgive me if I lie*
> *For they instructed me to live, not die.*
> *"Grief cannot compensate for what is lost,"*
> *They told me. "Win, and never mind the cost.*
> *Show to the world the face the world would see;*
> *Be slave, be pet, conceal your Self—but be."*

Lurking behind the docile Christian lamb,
Unconquered lioness asserts: "I am!"

POETS BEYOND THE BLUES

(In memory of Rosey E. Pool)

"I walk through the churchyard
    To lay this body down;
I know moon-rise, I know star-rise;
I walk in the moonlight, I walk in the starlight;
I'll lie in the grave and stretch out my arms,
I'll go to judgment in the evening of the day,
And my soul and thy soul shall meet that day,
    When I lay this body down."
                    (Negro Spiritual)

Some day we will remember how it was before you came.
Some day we will dare to face ourselves
in mirrors that do not lie
and be ashamed.

We were like particles of metal dust floating on stagnant air,
visible only in our separateness, until you rose among us
with a solar clarity that magnetized us
with your sharing of our pain.
Then we looked around
and saw that we were not alone.
We were one. And we were strong.

Some day we will remember
how much a part of us you came to be,
knowing our star-rise, walking in our moonlight,
laying your presence down among the corpses of our murdered dreams.

A native of Holland whose scholarship in Afro-American poetry began in 1925, Dr. Pool was imprisoned for underground opposition to Hitler's occupation, escaped, and lived hidden for nineteen months until the Liberation. On her first visit to the United States in 1959-60, she was instrumental in drawing together Black poets in various locations, including seven in Detroit who were later published in her anthology, *Beyond the Blues* (Kent, England: The Hand and Flower Press, 1962). Following the peak of the Civil Rights Movement, her motives were questioned by some of the younger Black militants.

45

POSTMORTEM

Who were you, really? Who are you now?
You always spoke in coded messages.
What were you trying to say?
Was it the real you who tormented me
     through mazes and nightmares
Or was it only the claw of death scratching
Those undecipherable graffiti on the walls?

I have to know. It is too late to run any more.
I did love you anyhow,
But leave the door ajar a little
So that I may witness the rites of passage
And know at last your terrible and ancient face.

EXITS AND ENTRANCES

Through random doors we wandered
into passages disguised as paradise
and out again, discarding,
embracing hope anew, discarding again:
exits and entrances to many houses.

Without joy we sang,
without grace we danced,
our hump-back rhythms colliding
with our sanity,
our beauty blanching in a hostile sun.

How should we, could we
sing our song in a strange land?

Through random doors we have come
home to our kingdom, our own battleground,
not with harps, not with trumpets even,
but armed with the invincible sword and shield
of our own names and faces.

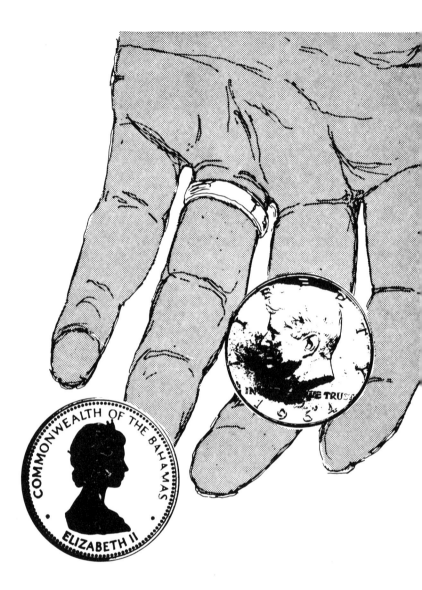

GOOD NEWS

(For Leonard)

The headlines never say goodmorning any more.
Every day the forecast reads: A chance of showers.
The Tigers keep losing the ballgames
And Dick Tracy is reported missing,
His smashed wrist-radio recovered
From a burned-out crater of the moon.
The market has plunged again;
Clad dimes and quarters have replaced the real ones.

Then you ring the doorbell with a Sunday sunrise
Rolled up casually in one pocket
And a handful of silver coins
With rare mintmarks in the other.

Clad coins are those which, originally made of silver, are now composed of copper
sandwiched between a cover of cupro-nickel, another base metal.

RELUCTANT SPRING

Early words flit through my mind's bare branches
looking for a cushion of leaves to nest in.
They carry bits of straw and dry debris
from leftover summers.

They cannot sing because their beaks are busy
holding on to fragments of the old for new foundations,
impatient to lay them down and bring their young
into the favor of the sun.

But April limps on crippled feet,
and though my robin scratches
in a patch of frozen sand
and another talon claws at my cranium,

I am at a loss to tell
where the worm hides all winter
and why the reluctant flowering of this season
requires the silence of a song.

CONQUEST

If it comes on like a cave man
I'll write it.

If it kicks down the door
I'll let it overcome me.

No polite knocking, no pleading, no
waiting to see if I'll let it in. I won't.

Unless it clubs me, subdues me,
drags me by my hair,

the poem
will never get written.

ECHOES

(For Duke Ellington)

The piano keys sit stiff and stark, sterile
as false teeth in a mouth
that no longer sings,
their black and white notes frozen
into cacophony of loss.

'I let a s-o-n-g go outa-my-heart'
and joy will never mount upon its wings
the same again.

But those perfect stones
tossed into timeless canyons
will reverberate in concentric melody
that will go on
        and on
            and . . . .

LOST   SONG

I lost a poem once.
Somehow I let it fall overboard
from a ship I was sailing.

I heard it splash, saw it ripple
like a silver fish in the moonlight
before the current carried it away.

I couldn't save it.
I couldn't even cry.

Sometimes I think I can still
hear it calling me, a frightened
helpless child lost

from the arms that would
have held it warm, wrenched
from the soul it would have healed.

Ever since, my ship has been
idling at half mast.

LYRIC

The songs don't sing any more.
They crawl or limp or stumble
over their own words
like drunken revelers
trying to find their way home
in the dark,
wailing to a street light
as if it were the moon.

Their wings don't sweep the skies.
They only flap a while in the noisy wind,
then fall back to low ground
where they peck like baffled chickens
at grains of discontent.

When
will the music start again?
When will the strong songs soar
and shimmer,
their bright black plumes dazzling
the golden morning
with melodies of light?

REQUIEM

Let my restless words flutter like autumn leaves
over my grave,
my unfinished pages whirl in a wind
of scarlet discontent.
When I lie blanketed in proper roses,
let my gaunt ghost rage into complacent twilights
scrawling across the hasty snow:
"To be continued."

ANONYMOUS WITNESS

(A Minor Christmas Vision)

(For Nick Hood, III)

I was asleep when the urgent message came.
I think I was dreaming, but so strong a dream
it was that I could not close my eyes again.
The palm trees moved complacently
in an imperceptible breeze, but I was not
complacent: There was somewhere I had to go.
                         I arose
and wrapped my robes around me.
The moon was gone, the faint stars had receded
into oblivion. Feeling more than seeing,
driven by a force I did not understand,
I saddled my camel in the sultry dark,
dusted the sand from my sandals
and mounted the reluctant beast. My companions
still lay sleeping in their tents.
In a few hours they would awake and wonder
where I had gone.

Where *was* I going? I did not even know.
But I rode, rode on in the midnight
in a heat of expectation, in a fever
of urgency, in a fury of compulsion. Until

all of a sudden such a starburst split the sky
that I leaped—or fell—from my camel in fear and dread
and sank to my knees in the sand.

When I dared to look up, I was startled by
flashes that fractured the inky night, signalling,
                        leading me on,
and I mounted the beast again and followed . . .

to a village . . . to a stable behind an inn.
A *stable*? To a mat of straw amid the smelly
docile cattle. Totally confused, I wondered,
"Mistake—or joke?" But as I turned to leave
in outrage, I saw three men approaching,
wearing royal robes and carrying expensive gifts.
I watched from a distance as they entered the barn
and knelt in deepest reverence. Whom
were they paying tribute to? He must have been
important. But I saw only a woman nursing a Baby
and it was as if they were worshipping this Child
with offerings of gold, perfume, and precious spices.

I was completely baffled. I knew at once
it was this scene I had been led to,
but I did not know what
                                    it was meant to mean.
When the three men from the East retired,
I too turned back toward the way I had come
and, suddenly weary, descended from my mount
and slept . . .

Again I dreamed—this time with clarity.
I saw this Child at two
                                    toddling toward His mother
with outstretched arms. An oblique dawnlight
cast His shadow in the form
                                    of a cross.
I saw Him again as a Boy preaching at Capernaum,
then as a Man riding a mule into Jerusalem. I heard
the thunder smite Golgotha's hill. I watched
the moon and stars go down in blood and sensed
a Father
            weeping for His little Boy,
weeping for the world.
I witnessed centuries of warfare and futility
chasing each other in circles, the kingdom
never coming. I heard the tale
told over and over again of the bright star
leading the wise men, leading me . . . but

it was the daylight after dark that lingered with me,
the whosoever-will, the I-am-the-Way-the-Truth-
and-the-Life, the come-unto-Me-
all-ye-who-are-weary, the
inasmuch-as-you-do-it-unto-these . . .

It was the star that led me
        to the beginning
but it was the dawning Sun that made me
        hopeful for the end.

WITHOUT

If I were blind and could not watch the late sun
melting into a simmering sea
or wish on the first starlight-starbright hope of evening,

it would not be the lost sunset
that would deprive me
but the oak-gold contour of your smile.

And your hand never rising in a benediction of heights
to which my earth-bound soul can never soar
(not the absence of a planet's borrowed light)
would leave me poor indeed.

If I were deaf, there is not a noble symphony that I would miss
so much as the melody of my name as you pronounce it.
Your slightest anger would put to shame
the most thunderous quaking of the earth.

Speak then, and let the earth revolve.
Smile, and let the oceans undulate.
If you did not sound or shine for me,
I could not be.

REFLECTION

The old man at the corner table
wears the face you will grow into.
I feel I should remember when the flesh
first started sagging and small lines
began to deepen around his mouth.
I notice the way he combs his hair
to cover up the balding middle, and I am sad.
He senses my naked stare
and our eyes clash, retreat
in recognition.

You swagger through the doorway
slightly out of breath and late as usual,
charming away my anger with the youthful
mischief of your indispensable smile.
I marvel again at your vibrant maleness
and the polished smoothness of your skin
stretched chestnut brown and taut across the fine
bones of your cheek and chin.
You unsettle the chair beside me
and I think of ancient African rivers
forever surging, forever replenishing
the world.

The man at the corner table rises
to leave. He fumbles with the credit card he needs
to tell him who he is.
Our eyes do not lock again
but the shadow of decay falls between us
as he moves away.

IMPRESSIONS

I.

And the blue dusk folded us into our narrow room
and the snow draped its silence across our window.
Behind our temporary door we sank into layers of deepening peace.

II.

We blew up promises like bright balloons
and sent them sailing on the festive air—
with strings attached.

III.

Suddenly unsheathed, the blade of morning
slashed our warm, pulsating darkness
into ribbons of pain.

DISCARDS

I emptied your wastebasket the other day
and found the star I gave you once
when we went walking on the air.

There was a seashell too.
I remember the morning I scraped
the crust of sand away
and handed you its pearl-dawn irridescence
to keep.

I started to save them for you
thinking you might some day regret
your haste in throwing them away.

But when I saw the gaudy bauble
that used to be my honest song
perched brazenly on your desk, I realized

that what the giver offers
gets altered sometimes in the passing
from heart to hand.

I tossed the shell and star
into my own wastebasket this afternoon.
The song will have to wait
until another day.

SEASONAL NOTE

Weeks
tumble over each other
like children in a lunch line
shoving ahead of slowpoke moments
to be first.

Is it really March already?
And here I am still dragging along
the carcass of an autumn fantasy—
a battered teddybear
I cannot put away.

In the end
it is the winter of The Record Snowfall
that everyone remembers, not the night
of miracle when
a bulb came on all by itself in the basement
of a deserted house.

DRIVING ALONG INTERSTATE 94

Suddenly rain
begins to dot the windshield.
The sun is caught
out in the open without a chance
to duck behind a cloud:
The devil is beating his wife again.
Soon I can hardly see the road.

Why don't I turn the switch
that sets the wiper blades
in therapeutic motion? Why do I
just sit here
hunched over the steering wheel
squinting at impenetrable
sheets of pain
as if I thought I knew
where I was going?

FENCES

Those barbed-wire summers
over which our memories dare not climb
for fear our jagged flesh remind us
we are mortal still

loom high between us as we turn apart
pursuing other summers
through easy-opening gateways
armed only with the cushioned
weapons of our pain.

AFTERTHOUGHT

I would like to believe we loved each other once—
that you were my Undiscovered Room
in a house full of mirrors and windows
and I, your paper Popperjack
snapped into small explosions from the folded air
to soar you into supersonic flight.

But the winds of many voices
have stretched you open to such constant height
that no rare single breath can lift you any more

and to tell the truth
my house has narrowed to such stifling darkness
that I no longer seek the hidden room,
only a door that opens outward
into a limitless expanse of light.

Kneeling Woman, from
the Baluba area, Congo.
Royal Museum of the
Belgian Congo,
Tervueren, Belgium

PACKRAT

My trouble is
I always try to save
everything

old clocks and calendars
expired words buried
in open graves

But hoarded grains of sand
keep shifting as rivers
redefine boundaries and seasons

Lengths of old string
rolled into neat balls
neither measure nor bind

nor do shelves laden with rancid sweets
preserve
what ants continually nibble away

Love should be eaten
while it is ripe
and then the pits discarded

Lord give me at last
one cracked bowl holding
absolutely nothing

About the Author

Born in Norfolk, Virginia, in 1923, Naomi Long Madgett spent her early years in East Orange, New Jersey, St. Louis, Missouri, and New Rochelle, New York. Following graduation from Virginia State College (now University), she was married and moved to Detroit, Michigan, where she still resides. A daughter was born of this first marriage.

After earning her master's degree at Wayne State University (now Wayne State), the author taught in the public high schools of Detroit for thirteen years. In 1968 she went to Eastern Michigan University as associate professor of English and retired as full professor in 1984. She was named professor-emeritus upon retirement. She also taught at The University of Michigan (Ann Arbor) and worked as a research associate at Oakland University. She holds a Ph.D. from The International Institute for Advanced Studies.

Like Phyllis Wheatley, Dr. Madgett began publishing early, her first collection appearing when she was seventeen years old. Her poems, which have been published or reprinted in many anthologies and journals in this country and abroad, were introduced in such publications as *The Poetry of the Negro, 1746-1949,* edited by Langston Hughes and Arna Bontemps (Doubleday, 1949) and *American Literature by Negro Authors,* edited by Herman Dreer (Macmillan, 1950). (Her early works were published under the names Naomi Cornelia Long and Naomi Long Witherspoon.)

The author is now married to Leonard P. Andrews and is mother of Jill Witherspoon Boyer, a poet and author of *Dream Farmer* and *Breaking Camp.* She is also a grandmother.